Teach Your Child to Read

A phonic reading guide for parents and teachers

Written by Annis Garfield

Illustrated by Jill Downie & Jane Gedye

✔Vermilion

2 3 4 5 7 9 10 8 6

First published in the United Kingdom in 1992 by
Vermilion, an imprint of Ebury Publishing
Random House UK Ltd.
Random House 20 Vauxhall Bridge Road
London SW1V 2SA

Random House Australia (Pty) Limited
20 Alfred Street, Milsons Point, Sydney,
New South Wales 2061, Australia

Random House New Zealand Limited
18 Poland Road, Glenfield,
Auckland 10, New Zealand

Random House (Pty) Limited
Isle of Houghton, Corner Boundary Road & Carse
O'Gowrie, Houghton 2198, South Africa

Random House Publishers India Private Limited
301 World Trade Tower, Hotel Intercontinental Grand
Complex, Barakhamba Lane, New Delhi 110 001, India

Random House UK Limited Reg. No. 954009
www.randomhouse.co.uk

A CIP catalogue record is available for this book from the
British Library.

ISBN 13: 9780091857400

Printed and bound in Thailand by Sirivatana Interprint Public Co., Ltd.

Papers used by Vermilion are natural, recyclable products
made from wood grown in sustainable forests.

Designed by Paul Burcher and Paul Burgess, Write Image Ltd.

Contents

Preface

You hold in your hands the key to teaching your child to read.

The beauty of the book's approach is that it is absolutely logical. It starts with the names and shapes of the letters of the alphabet and the sounds they represent. Then it moves on to short words, sentences, nursery rhymes, poems and stories – all of them delightfully illustrated. Within about six months, if you use the book as Annis Garfield intends, your child will be reading fluently.

Unaccountably, the teaching of reading has been an educational battleground for nearly 40 years. In that time, numberless children have been handicapped by being taught to guess at words by their shape and memorise them as if they were hieroglyphics. Annis Garfield, a firm traditionalist, has rediscovered the only method that works for every child.

John Clare
Education Editor
The Daily Telegraph
London

Introduction

Children, if they are to make progress in their education, in their career and in life generally, must learn to read fluently and well. They must learn to read without difficulties or problems. They must learn to read with enjoyment and confidence. The skill of reading is a child's passport to future work and leisure, for what can beat the satisfaction of a good book? An early, trouble-free mastery of reading is the greatest start a child can have; confidence in reading will inspire confidence in everything else. Conversely, children who do not learn to read well, fluently and with enjoyment carry a millstone round their neck throughout their education and a permanent handicap in life.

Difficulties of the English Language

Our glorious English language is a multilingual, multicultural hotch-potch of words of varied historical, geographical and ethnic origins, and of haphazard development. All this makes for a versatile and highly expressive language with a large vocabulary, but its intricacies also seem calculated to confuse. It is not, therefore, the straightforward, structured, orderly pattern of words we would choose as suitable for the first lessons for small children.

The various irregularities and inconsistencies of English must bewilder the child. How should he know that the word 'sign' comes from the Latin 'signum' and therefore has a 'g' which is now silent? How should he know that the odd word 'knee' can be explained by its common Teutonic origins with the Latin word 'genu' and the German 'knie'? French origins explain 'uncle', 'aunt', 'nephew' and 'niece'. 'Sugar' is from its Arabic forebear 'sukkar' via the French 'sucre'. 'Idea' and 'fancy' are from the Greek. 'Flu' comes from the Italian 'influenza'; 'cocoa' from Portuguese; 'coffee' from Malay; 'tattoo' from Polynesian; 'tobacco', 'potato' and 'toboggan' from American Indian; 'wrong', 'call', 'sky', 'take' and 'ill' from Scandinavian. Thus are some of the oddities in English spelling and pronunciation explained to us, perhaps, but they remain inexplicable to a child.

It is easy to see how the apparent inconsistencies in our language may present confusion and difficulties to the young child attempting to read it for the first time.

'Bead' and 'bread', 'said' and 'paid' presented to the child together, baldly and without explanation, can only cause confusion. These words must be presented in a graduated, phonetic order and sequence so as to be more easily assimilated by the child, more user-friendly. This is what this phonetic reading book sets out to do: to present every word in its due order so as not to confuse the child or contradict the phonetic rules suggested as useful initial guides.

How to Use this Book

This book presents the phonetic, step-by-step method of teaching reading. It is flexible. It can be taught by parents to one pre-school child, by teachers to a whole class or by parents to an older child in difficulties; it can also rescue children and adults with reading problems.

Steps to Reading

The first step in learning to read is to learn the letters of the alphabet. The child must learn to recognise, remember and distinguish the twice times twenty six symbols which make up our alphabet (the job of the first alphabet in Section 1). She must learn their names and the sounds they make, the first or basic sounds (the job of the second alphabet). The parent or teacher must not expect the letters to be known perfectly at once. Constant repetition together with the association of words and pictures will instil this knowledge.

Once the child is beginning to recognise her letters, she is ready to put together simple words with short vowel sounds (Section 2). Next, she can learn simple, two-syllable words, 's' endings, simple consonant combinations and some long vowels (Section 3). With this information, she will now be ready to meet further consonant combinations (Section 4), longer words, new vowel sounds and letter combinations (Section 5) and more difficult vowel sounds and words (Section 6). By the end of the book she will be able to read fluently.

The length and frequency of lessons and the rate of progress to be expected will vary according to the age, experience and circumstances of the child. Daily sessions of ten minutes or so will be sufficient for the pre-school child having individual lessons with a parent. The school-age child can take more and approximately six months of this system exclusively, correctly and regularly taught should see her reading.

The contents of this book have necessarily been condensed and abbreviated to keep within one manageable volume. The teacher may expand each lesson by giving the child more word lists and writing more sentences and stories. This will reinforce the lesson being learnt.

The older child, who has become confused and has developed problems with and a resistance to reading can be rescued by careful adherence to the principles of this primer. These principles cannot be emphasised too often – to learn the sounds of the letters; to spell out each word in its graded, classified order according to the suggested rules; constant repetition and practice. This method will work for all.

The Silent Letter
From Section 2, the child will meet silent letters, such as 'g' in 'gnat' and 'b' in lamb. Whenever words with silent letters occur, the teacher should spell the word out *without* them, e.g. l'a'm', and teach the child to ignore the silent letter. The teacher may also cover the silent letter with a piece of card, or cross through it with a pencil: lamb̸.

Teacher's Role
It is the task of the teacher:

● to call the letters by their sounds not names.

● to go on to the next page before the current one is completely mastered.

● not to expect the early sections to be learnt quickly.

● to encourage the child (by pointing to each letter with a pencil) to spell out each word letter by letter at first: m'a't', mat; then sound by sound: for the word 'skip' say sk'i'p', skip.

● constantly to be ready to help the child over difficulties by suggesting the right sound or word, by helping her to work it out syllable by syllable (this is the purpose of the hyphens in the word lists – to show where the word is to be broken up, to show how the word is to be tackled: la-bel, pi-lot, a-way, tun-nel, rab-bit).

● never to let the child become stuck but, if she hesitates, quickly to pronounce the letters for her.

● cheerfully to accept that some days are 'bad' days, to laugh and do something else.

● to start the book again sometimes.

● to let the child have a favourite page which is read over and over again.

● to read some old and some new material every day.

General Points
Children are not bored (an accusation often levelled) by the drill of phonetic wordlists and the simple reading text which at first is all they can manage. They are pleased to get it right and be praised. It may not be a meaningful,

stimulating story in the adults' eyes, but the child is learning and enjoying a skill which extends well beyond the activity of reading. She is learning to analyse and work problems out for herself; she is learning to use her reason, and stretch her mind; that and the right reading material is sufficient at this stage.

Meaningful, stimulating stories may be read *to* her but she must not be confused by being asked to read words for which she is not ready. The only words that are introduced before their due time in this book are key words such as 'the', 'my', and 'his', to help build simple sentences. Just tell the child how these words are to be sounded, adding that they will be properly dealt with later.

The essence of the phonetic system is the step-by-step progress through carefully arranged and exactly graduated reading material – *lists* of phonetically similar words with the relevant phonetic principle explained, together with accompanying *text* and *verse* incorporating the words just taught.

Great use is made of rhyming verses in this reading book and for many reasons. First, the lines may be short and simple and therefore attractive to the child and easy to read;

secondly, the rhyme often suggests the word:

Mary Arabella Sue
Lost a button off her shoe.

Nursery rhymes are or should be familiar to the child and this will help her reading of them and create a feeling of achievement when she can match the words on the page with the words in her head. But, most of all, poetry and rhyme is included for its own sake. Hurrah for its rollicking rhythms, its crystallised situations, its wit and wisdom, its words that fit. Most children will enjoy and remember poetry and benefit from learning verses by heart.

Finally it must be repeated that this phonetic arrangement of material is the best method of teaching reading. It has always worked faultlessly and with huge and universal success in the past. Heaven knows why it was ever abandoned!

Section

In this first section there are two arrangements of the alphabet; the first is to teach the child the shapes of the letters of the alphabet; the second is to teach the child the sounds they make.

Teacher's notes

The aim of the first alphabet is to teach the child to know the names and recognise the letters of the alphabet. The aim of the second alphabet is to teach the child their first or basic sound. For example, 'Aa' is called Aa (ay) but says 'a' (as in 'cat').

Do not expect any letter to be perfectly known at once. Constant repetition together with the association of words and pictures will instil this knowledge. The teacher should refer back to this section again and again.

Pay particular attention to the common confusion between various letters, such as 'b' and 'd' and 'p'.

Note: The text underneath each letter is to be read *to* the child. The child is *not* expected to read this text.

A

is like **A**lice reading in the **A**ttic

B

is like the **B**lackbird with a **B**right **B**eak

a

is like sir **a**rthur the **a**dder

b

is like a **b**at and **b**all

C **D** **E**

is like **C**olin **C**alling

is like **D**ave and **D**eb the **D**ancing **D**olphins

is like **E**thel's **E**legant **E**arring

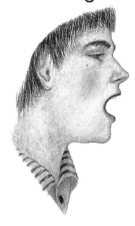  

c **d** **e**

is like **c**olin **c**alling

is like **d**avid the **d**iver

is like **e**ddie the **e**lastic **e**el

F   **G**   **H**

is like the **F**eathered **F**lamingo

is like **G**eoffrey the **G**entle **G**iraffe

is like **H**arry doing the **H**igh jump

f   **g**   **h**

is like a **f**ern

is like a **g**arland

is like **h**enry the **h**obby **h**orse

I

is like **I**an in a
rocket

J

is like the
Jellyfish

K

is like **K**evin
Kicking

i

is like **i**rma with an
idea

j

is like **j**asper the seal
juggling with a ball

k

is like a
key

L

is like a
Leg

M

is like **M**ark and **M**ike,
two **M**en **M**arching

N

is like **N**ails in a
piece of wood

l

is like a **l**ong stick of
liquorice

m

is like a
monster

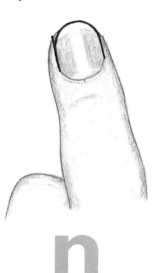

n

is like a
finger **n**ail

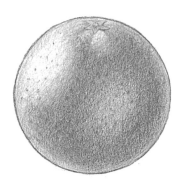

O

P

Q

is like an
Orange

is like **P**auline giving
Peter a **P**iggy-back

is like a **Q**uintuplet
Quintet singing carols

o

p

q

is like an
orange

is like **p**atsy with
a **p**igtail

is like a
queen

R

is like **R**ed **R**iding Hood
hiding from the wolf

S

is like the
Swan

T

is like a **T**ea
Table

r

is like a
rabbit

s

is like a
small **s**wan

t

is like **t**om at
the **t**urnstile

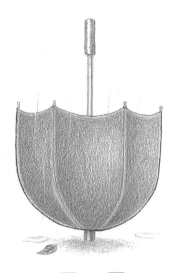

U

is like an
Umbrella

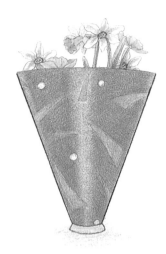

V

is like a
Vase

W

is like the
Waves

u

is like a small
umbrella

v

is like **v**ictor
wearing a **v**est

w

is like **w**ings

X

is like Alex's
X-ray

Y

is like **Y**asmin
Yawning

Z

is like **Z**achary
reading **Z**ealously

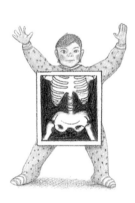

x

is like **x**avier's
x-ray

y

is like a **y**acht with
yellow sails

z

is like a **z**ig-**z**ag

Aa Bb Cc

Dd Ee Ff Gg Hh

Ii Jj Kk Ll Mm

Nn Oo Pp Qq Rr

Ss Tt Uu Vv Ww

Xx Yy Zz

A **a**nt

D **d**og

G **g**ate

B **b**ed

E **e**gg

H **h**at

C **c**at

F **f**rog

I **i**nk

jug

mug

pig

king

nose

queen

leg

orange

rabbit

S **s**un

V **v**an

Y **y**acht

T **t**ap

W **w**eb

Z **z**ip

U **u**mbrella

X bo**x**

Section

In this section, the child is introduced to simple words using each of the five vowels in turn, in their first or short sound: 'bat', 'bet', 'bit', 'bot', 'but'.

In addition to such three-letter words, the child will also meet the silent letter as in 'lamb', and in similar sounding short words ending in 'ck' (back) or in a double consonant (sill).

Teacher's notes

Each word must always be spelt out, i.e. voiced aloud sound by sound. The teacher should point with a pencil to the first letter, encouraging and, if necessary, helping the child to say the sound it makes; and so to the second letter on its own, and so on.

With the word van, for example, the teacher will point to the letter 'v' and encourage the child to say v$^/$ (not vee), then to say a$^/$ (not ay), then n$^/$ (not en), and finally the whole word van all together. Thus v$^/$ a$^/$ n$^/$, van.

When reading, always call the letters by their sounds, not their names. Silent letters may be crossed through with a pencil (ba¢k). Spell out the word without the silent letter.

Read each word three times, working across each row in turn from left to right.

Van	Can	Man	Ran
VAN	CAN	MAN	RAN
van	can	man	ran
Cat	Bat	Hat	Gnat
CAT	BAT	HAT	GNAT
cat	bat	hat	gnat
Ham	Jam	Ram	Lamb
HAM	JAM	RAM	LAMB
ham	jam	ram	lamb
Cap	Lap	Map	Tap
CAP	LAP	MAP	TAP
cap	lap	map	tap
Sad	Dad	Bad	Tab
SAD	DAD	BAD	TAB
sad	dad	bad	tab
Jazz	Back	Sack	Pack
JAZZ	BACK	SACK	PACK
jazz	back	sack	pack

Leg	Peg	Beg	Net	Met	Jet
LEG	PEG	BEG	NET	MET	JET
leg	peg	beg	net	met	jet

Pet	Wet	Web	Den	Hen	Men
PET	WET	WEB	DEN	HEN	MEN
pet	wet	web	den	hen	men

Pen	Wren	Ten	Keg	Meg	Egg
PEN	WREN	TEN	KEG	MEG	EGG
pen	wren	ten	keg	meg	egg

Bell	Yell	Well	Fell	Sell	Tell
BELL	YELL	WELL	FELL	SELL	TELL
bell	yell	well	fell	sell	tell

Bed	Fed	Led	Red	Wreck	Neck
BED	FED	LED	RED	WRECK	NECK
bed	fed	led	red	wreck	neck

Peck	Deck	Web	Hem	Mess	Less
PECK	DECK	WEB	HEM	MESS	LESS
peck	deck	web	hem	mess	less

Bin	Din	Tin	Win	Bit	Pit
BIN	DIN	TIN	WIN	BIT	PIT
bin	din	tin	win	bit	pit
Sit	Dig	Pig	Ill	Pill	Mill
SIT	DIG	PIG	ILL	PILL	MILL
sit	dig	pig	ill	pill	mill
Hill	Will	Hid	Kid	Lid	Lick
HILL	WILL	HID	KID	LID	LICK
hill	will	hid	kid	lid	lick
Pick	Kick	Sick	Lip	Zip	Nip
PICK	KICK	SICK	LIP	ZIP	NIP
pick	kick	sick	lip	zip	nip
Whip	Six	Mix	Fix	Kiss	Miss
WHIP	SIX	MIX	FIX	KISS	MISS
whip	six	mix	fix	kiss	miss
Hiss	Fizz	Whizz	Give	Live	Jim
HISS	FIZZ	WHIZZ	GIVE	LIVE	JIM
hiss	fizz	whizz	give	live	jim

Hog	Dog	Log	Jog	Mop	Cop
HOG	DOG	LOG	JOG	MOP	COP
hog	dog	log	jog	mop	cop
Top	Hop	Got	Cot	Hot	Dot
TOP	HOP	GOT	COT	HOT	DOT
top	hop	got	cot	hot	dot
Not	Knot	Pot	Ox	Fox	Box
NOT	KNOT	POT	OX	FOX	BOX
not	knot	pot	ox	fox	box
Boss	Toss	Moss	Mock	Sock	Cock
BOSS	TOSS	MOSS	MOCK	SOCK	COCK
boss	toss	moss	mock	sock	cock
Lock	Bob	Rob	Job	Cob	Cod
LOCK	BOB	ROB	JOB	COB	COD
lock	bob	rob	job	cob	cod
Rod	Pod	Nod	John	On	Off
ROD	POD	NOD	JOHN	ON	OFF
rod	pod	nod	john	on	off

Dug	Jug	Mug	Rug	Cut	Hut
DUG	JUG	MUG	RUG	CUT	HUT
dug	jug	mug	rug	cut	hut
Nut	But	Fun	Run	Sun	Bun
NUT	BUT	FUN	RUN	SUN	BUN
nut	but	fun	run	sun	bun
Gun	Tub	Cub	Pub	Sub	Sud
GUN	TUB	CUB	PUB	SUB	SUD
gun	tub	cub	pub	sub	sud
Mud	Cup	Pup	Bus	Fuss	Gull
MUD	CUP	PUP	BUS	FUSS	GULL
mud	cup	pup	bus	fuss	gull
Dull	Buzz	Fuzz	Puff	Cuff	Ruff
DULL	BUZZ	FUZZ	PUFF	CUFF	RUFF
dull	buzz	fuzz	puff	cuff	ruff
Hum	Mum	Gum	Sum	Dumb	Thumb
HUM	MUM	GUM	SUM	DUMB	THUMB
hum	mum	gum	sum	dumb	thumb

Can I have a cat, Dad?

Can I have a cat?

Dan has a cat.

Sam has a cat.

Ann has a cat.

Can I have a cat, Dad?

I can nag and nag till I have a cat.

I can have it on my lap, in a bag, in a sack.

My cat can be Tab.

Tab can have ham and jam in a pan.

Can I have a pig as well then, Dad?

Can I have a pig?

Let me have a pig.

A pig can live with Jen, the hen, and Tab, the cat.

My pig will be Miss Penny Pig.

Miss Penny Pig will live in a bin.

I have a big bin and it has a lid.

My cat, Tab.

Sat in his cab.

On his lap

He had his map.

And at the back

He had a sack.

In that sack Tab had a rat

And a bat

And a pan and a can

And a ram and a lamb

And a mat and a gnat

And a tap and a cap.

Jen, Jen,
The fat, red hen,
Fell in the well
And fell up again.

Can I have a hen then, Dad?
Can I have a hen?
Meg has a hen.
Let me have a fat, red hen as a pet.

My hen can be Jen.
Jen can peck at the sack.
'Well, have a hen, then,' said Dad.
'Less mess, I guess, a hen than a cat.'

Let me have a dog, Dad.

Tell me I can have a dog.

My dog will be Dot, the top dog.

But I will be the boss and Dot will do as I tell him.

Dot will sit if I tell him to sit.

Dot will get my cap if I tell him to get my cap.

Dot can have a box as his bed.

Let us have a cub, Mum.

It will be fun to have a fox cub.

My fox cub will be Rub-a-Dub.

He will run up the hill.

He will sit in the sun.

He can live in a den.

It is dull not to have a fox cub and a dog.

It is dull not to have a pal.

But I <u>have</u> got a hen.

Dan, Dan,
The big, bad man,
He fell in a pit;
Let him get up if he can.

Ann, Ann,
Had a fan.

Ben, Ben,
met ten men.

Bill, Bill,
He fell ill.

John, John,
His sock is on.

Gus, Gus,
Got off the bus.

All work and no play,
Makes Jack a dull boy.

Section

In this section the child meets the final 's'; long vowels combined with silent letters; two-syllable simple words and two-syllable words ending in 'y'.

He will also meet the effect of 'r' on vowels; consonant combinations with 's', 'r' and 'l'; long vowels are also introduced.

Teacher's notes

Explain the phonetic principle of each lesson:

(p.38) the final 's' – the child should be taught to say $b^/a^/g^/s^/$, bags.

(p.40) long vowels – the child should be taught to say $j^/a^/$ (long 'a'), 'jay'; $b^/e^/$ (long 'e'), 'bee'. Remember silent letters.

(p.42) hyphens teach the child where to break up two-syllable words. Tackle a word bit by bit. Cover the second part of a word to help the child to work out the first part.

(p.46) how vowels have a different sound when followed by 'r', ('hem' and 'her', 'sit' and 'sir', 'not' and 'nor').

(p.54ff) 'magic e' on the end of a word makes the preceding vowel long, ('at' and 'ate', 'rip' and 'ripe'). Vowels can also become long when combined with other vowels ('man' and 'main', 'set' and 'seat').

Jen the Hen

(Final 's')

bags   cogs
gags   dogs
rags   jogs
tags   logs
wags

      bugs
begs   hugs
eggs   jugs
legs   mugs
pegs   rugs

digs
figs
pigs
rigs

Ben has lots of vans.
Ann has lots of jets.
It's fun when Ben lets
His vans mix with Ann's.

John has a box
With his pet, red fox.
His bed is John's socks;
If he runs, the box rocks.

Jen the Hen lives in a pen.

Jen the Hen sits and sobs in the pen.

'Oh, oh, oh,' sobs Jen the Hen.

'It is dull to sit in a pen.

It is no fun to peck at bugs in the pen.

My pals the rats can live in huts and in tubs.

My pals the pigs can sit in mud, can dig in pits and have lots of fun.'

'My pals the dogs can run up hills and sit on rugs.

My pals the fox cubs can sit on logs in the sun and have fun.

I sit in a pen. I am sad. It is no fun. It is dull.

Let me run with them.'

But Mr Hen Man will not let Jen the Hen run on the hills.

Pals to tea

(Long vowels with silent letter)

bay	die
day	high
jay	lie
lay	pie
may	sigh
pay	tie
ray	
say	bow
way	go
	Joe
bee	know
he	low
key	mow
me	no
see	so
tea	
we	do
	Sue
	you
	who

'Well,' says Jen the Hen, 'it's a hot day and I see a way I can have fun. I will have my pals to tea. I will have Tab the Cat, Miss Penny Pig, Dot the Dog and Rub-a-Dub the Fox Cub to tea. We will have tea at six. That will be fun. And I can see Tab the Cat by my hen run. I will tell him.

'Hello, Tab the Cat,' yells Jen the Hen. 'Tab the Cat, will you come to tea? I will buy buns. I will buy ham. I will buy jam. I will buy pie. We will have eggs. I will get my big teapot so we can have lots of cups of tea.

'Will you tell Miss Penny Pig to come to tea with me at six? Will you go and see Dot the Dog and Rub-a-Dub the Fox Cub and tell them to come to tea with me?'

Betty Bun,
If you've done
Some super sums,
Then come to tea with me.

But, Betty Bun,
If it's none
That you've done,
If you've not done one,
You cannot come with me.

Toby Robot
Cannot go,
If you do not
Tell him so.

No tea

(Two-syllable words)

bon-net	can-not
pock-et	par-rot
pack-et	car-rot
jack-et	cam-el
buck-et	ken-nel
tick-et	tun-nel
pig-let	fun-nel
	pet-rol
rib-bon	
but-ton	rab-bit
cot-ton	vis-it
les-son	
bot-tom	lab-el
rob-in	li-on
	ba-con
kit-ten	pi-lot
mit-ten	ri-ot
bit-ten	o-pen
hid-den	
sud-den	

So Tab the Cat runs off to tell Jen the Hen's pals, Miss Penny Pig, Dot the Dog and Rub-a-Dub the Fox Cub, to come to tea.

'Well,' says Dot the Dog, 'it is a hot day. It is not wet. I am glad to come to tea with Jen the Hen.'

Miss Penny Pig says, 'Oh, I will get my red bonnet with the red ribbon. That will be fantastic.'

Rub-a-Dub the Fox Cub says, 'I am glad to come to tea with Jen the Hen. Ham and eggs, did you say? That will be fantastic. It will not be bad to sit in the sun in Jen the Hen's hen run and have ham and eggs and sip tea. Yes, I will come.'

But when Tab the Cat, Miss Penny Pig, Dot the Dog and Rub-a-Dub the Fox Cub get to Jen the Hen's pen they cannot get in. Jen the Hen cannot open the pen. Bad Mr Hen Man has a lock on Jen the Hen's pen. Bad Mr Hen Man has hidden the key. Jen the Hen cannot unlock the pen.

'I have no key,' says Jen the Hen. 'I cannot let you in.'

'I have a key in my pocket,' says Dot the Dog. 'This key may fit the lock.' But Dot the Dog cannot open the pen with his key. His key will not fit in the lock.

'I can open a lock with a pin,' says Tab the Cat. Miss Penny Pig has a packet of pins in a bag in her pocket. 'Let me give you one of my pins,' says Miss Penny Pig. But none of the pins will open the lock on the pen.

Tab the Cat, Miss Penny Pig, Dot the Dog and Rub-a-Dub the Fox Cub sit by the pen. They cannot get in to have tea with Jen the Hen. 'Oh, oh, oh, I am so sad,' Jen the Hen sobs. 'I am in a mess.'

The tunnel

(Two-syllable words ending in 'y')

Dad-dy   luck-y
hap-py   ug-ly
Jack-y   bun-ny
Sam-my   fun-ny
          sun-ny
Pen-ny   hur-ry
Vick-y
lil-y   ba-by
sil-ly   la-dy
Kit-ty   A-my
pit-y   dai-sy
diz-zy   la-zy

hob-by   ea-sy
bod-y
fog-gy   i-vy
hol-ly   ti-dy
jol-ly
lol-ly   ho-ly
pop-py   po-ny
lor-ry   ro-sy
sor-ry
          beau-ty

Jen the Hen has a big, red bonnet.

Is she well today?

No. Jen the Hen is sad and sick.

She has hidden in the hay.

In the pocket
Of my jacket
Is a ticket
For the bus.

If you have
A ticket, Janet,
You can come
With us.

Billy, I'm sorry
You fell off the lorry.
But isn't it lucky
You didn't get mucky?

40

'It is OK, Jen the Hen,' say Tab the Cat and Miss Penny Pig. 'Do not sob. Do not be unhappy. We cannot unlock the pen, so we will dig a tunnel to get you out.'

They begin to dig a big tunnel into Jen the Hen's pen. It is a big job. It is not an easy job. Tab the Cat has a pick and he digs into the rock with it. Miss Penny Pig fills a bucket with bits and tips them into a pit.

Rub-a-Dub the Fox Cub unbuttons his jacket. 'Oh, I am hot,' he sighs. 'So am I,' says Dot the Dog.

Tab the Cat suddenly gets very bossy. 'Quick, quick, you dozy dog,' he yells. 'Do not be lazy. Get into the tunnel and dig.'

'Do not tell me I am lazy and dozy,' Dot the Dog yells back to Tab the Cat. 'Nobody digs as quickly as I do.'

'Oh,' says Tab the Cat, 'I am very sorry. I am in a tizzy. Mr Hen Man will come and see the tunnel. He will come in a tick, I know he will. That will not be funny.'

Jen the Hen runs away

(Effect of 'r' on vowels)

bar	let-ter	ba-ker
car	bet-ter	pa-per
far	bit-ter	fe-ver
jar	but-ter	le-ver
tar	en-ter	po-ker
gar-den	sis-ter	mo-tor
mar-ket	mis-ter	o-ver
car-pet	win-ter	
	din-ner	
her	sum-mer	
fir	ham-mer	
sir	sup-per	
girl	cop-per	
fur	nev-er	
hurt	ev-er	
hurl	riv-er	
	rob-ber	
or	rub-ber	
for	lad-der	
nor	un-der	
cor-ner	doc-tor	

Suddenly, Miss Penny Pig pops up out of the tunnel. Suddenly, Miss Penny Pig enters Jen the Hen's hen run. Tab the Cat and Dot the Dog follow; then Rub-a-Dub the Fox Cub, as muddy and dirty as can be.

'Well done,' says Jen the Hen. 'Well done. You have dug far under my pen so I can get out. I have never got out of my horrid, dirty hen run before. Forget the tea. Forget the buns and jam. They do not matter. I am sorry, but it is better for me to run away.'

But then, suddenly, Miss Penny Pig begins to yell. 'Quick, quick, I can see Mr Hen Man. Mr Hen Man can see Jen the Hen. He can see the tunnel. He is mad.

'But see, by the corner, a big, red lorry. Can we get into the back of the lorry? Can we be hidden under the paper sacks? Well, we can have a go. Into the back of the lorry, everybody. Lie low until Mr Hen Man has gone away.'

When I am big
I'll have a car,
A big car,
A red car.
And in it I will go as far
As far as Africa.

Never, never
Go under a ladder
Or you will have bad luck.

Never, never
Swim over a river
Unless you can swim like a duck.

Runaway lorry

(Consonant combinations with 's')

stag	slug
stab	slap
step	slam
stick	slim
still	slip
stiff	slop
stop	slow
stuff	
stay	snap
star	sniff
start	snore
stir	snow
sty	snug
skip	speck
skim	spell
skin	spill
scar	spin
skirt	spot
scan	
scab	sway
	swim

It is bad luck for Jen the Hen, Tab the Cat, Miss Penny Pig, Dot the Dog and Rub-a-Dub the Fox Cub that the lorry is on a hill. For the lorry will not stop still on the hill. It will not stay on the hill. It will not stick to its spot on the hill. Oh, no. As Jen the Hen and the rest step into the back of the lorry, a sudden jerk starts it off.

'Oh, oh, oh,' yell Jen the Hen and Tab the Cat.

'Whoa, whoa, whoa,' yell Miss Penny Pig and Dot the Dog.

'Stop, stay, sit,' yells Rub-a-Dub the Fox Cub. 'Stop, stay, sit, you stupid lorry.'

The lorry hurls them to and fro, to and fro. And then they see the river at the bottom of the hill; they see they are on the way to the river.

'Stop, go slow, big, red lorry, we beg you. Do not spill us into the slippy, sloppy river.'

In the corner
Of my garden
Live two spiders
Spick and Span.

They spin a web
They spin it well.
See it
If you can.

Hop, skip and run
Hop, skip and run.
Lessons are over
Lessons are done.

Freddy the Frog

(Consonant combinations with 'r')

grub
grow
gra-vy
gruff
grim
grip
a-gree

crab
crack
cram
cry
cress
crib
crop
cross

free
fry
from
frog
fret
fro-zen

brick
brag
brim
brat
bro-ther

trap
tray
tree
true
try
trick
trim
trot
trac-tor

drum
drop
drip
drill
dress
drag
dry

press
pray
pry
prick
prim
pram
prom-ise
prob-lem
a-pric-ot

I am a frog from Frinton,
You are a crab from Cray.
Pray, drip me a drop
Of that apricot slop
And let me get on my way.

My dog and cat
Do not agree.
'Only one boss
And that is me,'
Said the dog.

'No, me,' spat the cat,
'And that's that.'

Freddy the Frog sits on his lily pad under a tree on the river. It is hot. It is sunny.

'Yippee,' says Freddy the Frog. 'I have a day off today. I will trim the cress in my river garden. I will be cross if greedy grubs have come to scoff the lot. I grow cress for me, not for greedy grubs. And then I will flop into the river for a swim.

'I will have my dinner on a tray on my lily pad and then I will lie in the sun and snore for the rest of the day.'

But Freddy the Frog never gets his day to relax. Suddenly, CRACK, BAM, WHAM, a horrid din from high up on the hill; and then Freddy the Frog sees a mad, runaway lorry. It skips, it skids, it spins on its way to the river.

'Stop, stop, let us out,' comes the cry from the lorry.

'This is horrid. I will stop this lorry if I can,' says Freddy the Frog. Then he yells to them all in the lorry, 'Do not panic. I will free you. I will get to grips with this problem lorry.'

A narrow miss

(Consonant combinations with 'l')

fly	blot
flee	blue
flag	blow
flat	bled
flap	black
flock	blab
flip	block
flit	bless
plum	clock
play	clap
plan	click
plod	clip
pluck	cliff
plug	clod
plen-ty	club
	clay
glad	clat-ter
glow	clev-er
glue	
glum	

So Freddy the Frog has to forget his free day.

'Blow my day off,' he mutters. 'Big flap on with this lorry. Got to get a plan to stop this crazy lorry before it kills them all. Must do my bit. Hurry, hurry, hurry.'

Flip, flap, flip, flap, as he hops quickly across the lily pad. Slip, slop, slip, slop. Then he flaps his flippers, snaps his back legs, clicks his forelegs and, with a big jump, drops plumb into the cab of the runaway lorry.

Freddy the Frog tries to grab the controls to stop the lorry.

'Oh, oh, oh,' he cries. 'I do not know the stop button. If I am clever I will press the correct button and the lorry will stop. Is it this red button? Or is it this black button? Or is it that blue button? I will try this red one and see.'

Freddy the Frog gets his thumb on a red button. The lorry skids to a stop. It stops by a tree on a cliff. Over the cliff is a big drop. 'A narrow miss,' sighs Freddy the Frog.

I have plenty of plums in my garden;

I have plenty of bricks in my box.

I am glad I'm so clever

I'll be clever for ever

And dress every day in blue socks.

On Granny's skirt I stuck some glue;

It was a stupid thing to do.

The problem is she's very stuck.

She sat down and cannot get up.

Brave Freddy the Frog

('Magic e' and 'i' making long 'a')

cake	spade	rain
bake	aid	lane
lake	paid	stain
make	laid	train
take	fade	plain
wake	wade	plane
stake	trade	cane
snake	blade	vain
fake	grade	
flake		same
rake	ape	name
	tape	lame
hail	grape	came
fail	cape	game
nail		flame
sail	gate	frame
tail	hate	dame
wail	date	
trail	late	brave
jail	skate	save
snail	crate	safe
frail		

Jen the Hen, Miss Penny Pig, Tab the Cat, Dot the Dog and Rub-a-Dub the Fox Cub come out of the back of the lorry. They are all in a state. They are all pale and grim.

Tab the Cat comes up to Freddy the Frog. 'Tell me your name,' he says. 'You were very brave to save us. It was clever of you to save us. We are all very grateful.'

'Oh, Freddy the Frog, you are fantastic,' says Miss Penny Pig. 'You are fantastic to press the stop button and save us. We are safe. I will not wail. We are safe.'

'Do not make a fuss,' says Freddy the Frog. 'Do not make a fuss. I am glad I came to your aid. I am glad I did not fail. I had to make a plan to save you. I had to make a quick plan. It was as plain as plain to see that I had to make a big jump to stop the lorry. It was plain that I had to jump into the cab to stop the lorry. I am glad I did not fail.'

The rain
In Spain
Rains mainly
On the plain.

Pat a cake
Pat a cake
Baker's man
Bake me a cake
As fast as you can.
Prick it and pat it
And mark it with 'B'
And put it in the oven
For baby and me.

Kate, Kate,
I know you'll be late.
Daisy and Amy
Will wait at the gate.
<u>Do</u> get your skates on.
<u>Don't</u> get in a state;
Oh, Kate, Kate, Kate!

Trip to Spain

(Long 'e' from 'ee' and 'ea')

reed   leaf
need   beef
feed   reef
speed
weed   leap
read   weep
lead   deep
       sweep
beam   peep
team   steep
steam
cream   green
dream   lean
gleam   clean
       mean
beak   queen
weak   been
speak   seen
leak
leek   meal
week   kneel
       feel
       real

Pussy cat, pussy cat,

Where have you been?

I've been up to London

To look at the Queen.

Emmeline

Has not been seen

For more than a week. She slipped between

The two tall trees at the end of the green...

We all went after her. 'Emmeline!'

'Emmeline,

I didn't mean-

I only said that your hands weren't clean.'

We went to the trees at the end of the green...

But Emmeline

Was not to be seen.

Then Jen the Hen begins to open her beak to speak.

'Please let me tell you, Freddy the Frog, that I have run away from horrid Mr Hen Man. These pals came to lead me out of my dirty pen by a tunnel. Horrid Mr Hen Man cannot keep me in that dirty pen. My pals have taken me away.'

'Oh, it did not seem that we were to escape from Mr Hen Man. We got into the back of the lorry and got under some sacks, but the lorry began to run away as it was on a hill. Oh, it was as if I was in a bad dream. The lorry began slowly, but then as the hill got steeper it sped faster and faster on its way to the deep, deep river.'

'Oh, my legs feel weak. I need to lean on that tree. But I have run away and I will never go back. I will never return.'

'And I am so grateful to you, Freddy the Frog, and to my pals as well, I will take you all on a treat. I will take you all to Spain by train for a week. We need a holiday, so let's go for a week to Spain on a train.'

A train ride to Spain

(Long 'i' from 'magic e' at the end of a word)

hide	crime	bite
ride	dime	kite
side	lime	quite
tide	slime	site
wide	time	white
knife	fine	ar-rive
life	mine	dive
wife	vine	drive
	wine	five
bike		hive
like	pipe	
spike	swipe	
	wipe	
file		
mile	sur-prise	
smile	wise	
stile	prize	
tile	size	

'To Spain?' they all cry. 'Ride inside a train to Spain? Oh, what fun. Why not?'

So Jen the Hen goes to buy the tickets for the trip to Spain.

'Five tickets, please,' she says to the ticket man. 'Oh, no, sorry, I mean six, not five; one for Freddy the Frog, one for Tab the Cat, one for Miss Penny Pig, one for Dot the Dog and one for Rub-a-Dub the Fox Cub; and mine makes six.'

'I like this train,' says Miss Penny Pig. 'I like a white train and the green line on the side makes it seem very fine. Oh, and see it has its name on the side, the White Rider.'

The train driver steps into his cab. 'We had better get in,' says Jen the Hen.

The train driver says, 'My name is Mike and my co-driver is Bill.'

Leg over
Leg over
The dog went to Dover.
He came to a stile
And hop he went over.

To market, to market
To buy a fat pig;
Home again, home again,
Jiggety jig.

I like my bike;
I ride for miles,
And everyone who sees me
Smiles.

On the train

(Long 'o' from 'magic e' and from 'oa')

load	groan	oat
road	moan	boat
toad	bone	coat
code	lone	goat
rode	stone	moat
	tone	note
oak	zone	vote
cloak		wrote
croak	soap	
joke	grope	cove
smoke	hope	stove
spoke	rope	wove
	slope	
coal		
foal	close	
hole	nose	
pole	rose	
	doze	
foam	froze	
roam		
dome		
home		

'Load all your stuff into the train. Load your cases, bags, hats and coats,' says Jen the Hen.

'Oh, oh, oh,' Freddy the Frog moans. 'My family at home will not know that I am off to Spain. Oh, Mr Porter, if I write a note will you take it to Mr Toad? Mr Toad has his home by my home. Mr Toad will see that my family are all well while I am away in Spain.'

Then the train begins to go.

'We will be on this train for a long time,' says Jen the Hen. 'I hope this will not seem horrid.'

'Horrid?' cry Tab the Cat and Dot the Dog. 'Oh, no, a train ride can never be horrid. We can play games. We can tell jokes. Miss Penny Pig can tell us a story. Miss Penny Pig is a super story teller.

'And then we can see out of the window. We can see the rabbit holes and see the baby rabbits run in and out of the rabbit holes as we clatter by. We can see rivers and canals with boats. We can see ducks as they float by the reeds. We can see the trees and roads and cars.'

'Well,' says Jen the Hen. 'Close the window now, please, someone. I am frozen. I am frozen to the bone. I hope that it will be hotter in Spain.' But no one speaks. No one makes a reply to Jen the Hen. Jen the Hen alone is awake. Snores come from the nose of Miss Penny Pig. Snores come from the noses of everybody.

'Well,' mutters Jen the Hen, 'if they are all asleep, then I will have a doze.' And as Jen the Hen opens her beak to say this and that to the driver before her nap ...zzz... Jen the Hen suddenly falls asleep.

A tune on the train

(Long 'u' from 'magic e' and from 'ui')

cube   fruit
tube   suit

nude
rude

duke
Luke

mule
rule
ruler

June
tune

use

brute
cute
flute
duty

Some time later the train comes to a sudden stop. Outside the window a cute kitten in a beautiful blue coat begins to play a tune on a flute. They all wake up.

'We are not in Spain yet, I am afraid,' says Jen the Hen. 'Not in Spain yet.'

'Is that a flute?' says Tab the Cat. 'Can I see a cute kitten in a beautiful blue coat? Can a kitten play a flute so well? Can a kitten play a tune on the flute so well? It is absolutely super. I have never heard a kitten play the flute.'

And Tab the Cat begins to hum the tune.

'It is a bit rude of Tab the Cat to hum and hum that tune,' complains Dot the Dog. 'I cannot get back to sleep. He hums and hums and that keeps me awake. It is very rude. I do not mean to complain, but it is rude of him to hum and keep me awake.'

Just then a goat comes on the train with a tray of fruit. 'Buy my fruit. Plums for sale. Ripe plums. Melons for sale. Ripe melons.'

'I will buy ten plums and five melons, please,' says Miss Penny Pig to the goat. And Miss Penny Pig gropes in her bag for a knife and plate and begins to cut up the plums and melons for everyone.

'Will you have a bit of plum or a cube of melon, Freddy the Frog?' says Miss Penny Pig. 'You may use my knife to cut it up more. Use my knife if you like, but please do not drop it.'

The duck has got a gun and shot -
The duck-hunter has gone to pot.

Row, row, row the boat
Gently down the stream;
Merrily, merrily, merrily, merrily,
Life is but a dream.

I can hop
And I can run;
My day is
A lot of fun.

Matthew, Mark, Luke and John
Bless the bed that I lie on.

This is the way the ladies ride:
Trit-trot, trit-trot, trit-trot, trit-trot;
This is the way the gentlemen ride:
Canter, canter, canter, canter;
This is the way the farmers ride:
Gallopy, gallopy, gallopy, gallopy
Down into the ditch!

Section 4

This section introduces further initial consonant combinations, the final 'nd', the initial and final 'sh' and words starting with 'wh' and 'wa'.

The child also meets the final 'r' plus consonant, 'th', 'ei' and 'ey', more final consonant combinations, 'ch' and 'tch' and the final 'ng' and 'nk'.

Teacher's notes

Explain to the child:

how to tackle new words, pointing to the letters to be taken together, i.e. scr'a'p', scrap.

how 's' and 'h' are sounded together as one sound: 'sh'.

similarly how 'w' and 'h' can make one sound: 'wh'.

how 'a' after 'w' can sound like 'o' as in 'was' and 'wash'.

that 't' and 'h' together sound 'th'.

that 'ei' and 'ey' sound as in 'rein' and 'they'.

Constant reminders must be given about silent letters to enable the child to tackle such words as 'neighbour' which, if the silent letters are marked and the word broken up, is quite straightforward – neigh-bour.

See out of the train

(Initial consonant combinations and final 'nd')

scrap	twelve
scrape	twenty
scraper	twig
scream	twin
screen	twit
scrub	be-tween

sprain	and
sprat	band
spray	hand
sprig	sand
	stand

stray	
streak	end
stream	bend
street	lend
stride	mend
strip	
stripe	bond
	fond
	pond

Jack Spratt did eat no fat;
His wife did eat no lean;
And so between them both,
you see,
They licked the platter clean.

I scream,
You scream,
We all scream
For ice cream.

'Well,' says Jen the Hen, as they all eat the bits of plum and the cubes of melon that Miss Penny Pig cuts up for them with her knife. 'It is lucky we are all pals. As we all get on so well, our trip to Spain will be great fun. No scraps, no screams, no strain between us.

'But let me tell you this: if you scrap or scream I will pick you up by the scruff of your neck and drop you out of the window. I will drop you on to the line below. We will have no strain on this train.'

'Yes,' they all reply. 'Yes, Jen the Hen. We are not twits. We will not scrap and be silly.'

'Oh,' says Tab the Cat. 'Out of the window I can see twin lambs. One of the twin lambs has run away from the flock. Oh, it is by a stream. Oh, it has stepped over the stream and trotted away. Oh, it has stopped to eat a twig from this tree and then a scrap more twig and then a sprig from that tree as it trots by.'

Story on the train

(Initial and final 'sh'; 'wh'; and 'a' after 'w')

shade	shred	rad-ish
shad-ow	shrug	van-ish
shag-gy		pol-ish
shake	cash	pun-ish
shal-low	crash	
shape	dash	wheel
shed	flash	wheat
sheep	rash	while
sheet	flesh	white
shell	dish	whine
shel-ter	dish-es	whale
shine	fish	whip
ship	wish	whisp-er
shiv-er	wish-es	
shock	brush	was
shop	crush	wasp
shore	gush	wash
shot	hush	want
show	rush	what
shy		wand
		wand-er

Then, Jen the Hen says, 'Hush, please hush, I have an idea. I have an idea of what we can do while the train rushes on and on. What we can do is tell stories. Miss Penny Pig, you may go first.'

And so Miss Penny Pig begins. She sits up. She wipes her nose. She brushes some white crumbs from her lap. She scrapes the mud off her trotters and then she rubs and polishes and shines her trotters.

'That's better,' she says. 'Now I can begin my story. But let me sit out of the shade. I do not want to sit in the shade. I want to sit in the sun. Tab the Cat, please will you swap seats so I can sit in the sun to tell my story.'

'Well,' mutters Dot the Dog, 'if she does not start soon we shall be in Spain. Hurry up and begin, please, Miss Penny Pig.'

I have a little shadow

That goes in and out with me.

And what can be the use of him

Is more than I can see.

He is very, very like me

From the heels up to the head;

And I see him jump before me,

When I jump into my bed.

She sells

Sea shells

On the sea shore.

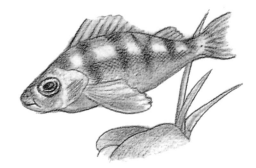

How happy to be a fish;

To dive and skim,

To dart and float and swim

And play.

Miss Penny Pig's story

(Final 'r' plus consonant)

bark	art
dark	cart
lark	dart
mark	part
mark-et	smart
park	tart
shark	
spark	fort
	port
cork	short
fork	sort
pork	sport
stork	
	dirt
lurk	shirt
Turk	squirt
turk-ey	hurt
jerk	
perk	
work	

At the start of my life I lived at home with my family. I had lots of brothers and sisters at home. My name, as you know, is Penny, and the others' names were Skylark, Curly, Corky, Smarty, Sparky and Cartwheel.

We lived in a park, Green Park. One end of Green Park was very smart. All sorts of families lived in Green Park. Apart from pig families like us, lots of storks lived by the pond. My pal Stan Stork used to stand on one leg in the pond for days and days on end. He used to stay on one leg in the pond.

'Aren't you bored?' I said to Stan one day. 'Why do you wait, Stan?'

'I have to wait,' he replied. 'You see, I hope to get a fish for supper.'

My brothers and sisters and I were very fond of sport. We played all sorts of games and sports in the park. We were very fond of every sport – tennis, cricket, netball, hockey, darts and football.

We liked football most, and the Pig family played as a team. We were the Piggy Porkers football team. That was the name of the team, the Piggy Porkers.

We were very smart in blue and white striped shirts and blue and white striped shorts. That was what we wore when we played.

Football team

(More final 'r' plus consonant)

barn	fern	horn
darn	burn	born
yarn	turn	worn
yard	earn	torn
hard	learn	corn
guard	earth	corn-flake
harp	bird	horse
sharp	third	course
arm	word	
a-larm	herd	
farm	heard	
farm-er	kerb	
harm	herb	
part-ner	dis-turb	
starve	girl	
carve	whirl	
half	pearl	
calf	purse	
	nurse	
	verse	
	worse	

The Piggy Porkers football team played football very well. I am not a show-off. It is true. We did play well.

We used to train hard. We even had a trainer to make us work hard to keep fit. His name was Herbie the Blackbird and five times every week Herbie the Blackbird made us train in a barn in the park.

It was great fun in the barn. We had a stove to burn logs in the winter and so we did not freeze while we trained. Herbie made us skip and run on the spot to get us all fit.

If we wanted to be in his Piggy Porkers football team we had to train very, very hard to be fit.

Little Boy Blue
Come blow up your horn.
The sheep's in the meadow,
The cow's in the corn.

Bell Horses, Bell Horses,
What time of day?
One o'clock, two o'clock,
Three and away.

There was a little girl
And she had a little curl
Right in the middle of her forehead.
And when she was good
She was very, very good,
But when she was bad
She was horrid.

I love little pussy
Her coat is so warm.
And if I don't hurt her
She will do me no harm.

Team training

('th' and 'ei')

the	throne
these	throat
those	throw
this	three
that	thrill
than	thrush
them	thrash
then	through
though	
	truth
bathe	teeth
breathe	faith
clothe	birth
clothes	cloth
with	
wheth-er	rein
	vein
thin	they
thick	o-bey
thumb	neigh
thirst-y	neigh-bour
thir-teen	eight
Thurs-day	weight

Every Monday and Thursday in the summer Herbie the Blackbird, our team trainer, made us go for a run through the park.

'This is your programme,' Herbie used to say. 'I have made you a programme to get you fit for your football games:

'Monday, run; Tuesday, skip; Wednesday, swim; Thursday, run again; Friday, shoot goals; and Saturday, a real game.

'And if you all stick to this programme, no team will beat you. If you all stick to this programme through thick and thin, you will beat every team that plays against you. If you grit your teeth, then you will thrash them. That is the truth, Piggy Porkers, you will beat them all.

'Oh, yes. You can have Sunday off as a treat. You can wash your games clothes on Sunday.'

One, two, three, four, five,
Once I caught a fish alive.
Six, seven, eight, nine, ten,
Then I let it go again.

Why did you let it go?
Because it bit my finger so.
Which finger did it bite?
This little finger on the right.

Little Blue Ben, who lives in the glen,
Keeps one blue cat and one blue hen,
Which lays of blue eggs a score and ten;
Where shall I find that little Blue Ben?

Lucy Locket lost her pocket,
Kitty Fisher found it;
Not a penny was there in it
But a ribbon round it.

Fed up

(More final consonant combinations)

lamp	tent	risk
camp	sent	lift
damp	spent	gift
stamp	went	tuft
limp	twen-ty	left
lump	belt	
bump	felt	ant
jump	knelt	pant
thump		print
	desk	print-er
nest	next	hunt
best	kept	hunt-er
west	slept	
fist		big
mist	sense	big-ger
wrist		big-gest
dust	milk	hot
must	silk	hot-ter
trust	tilt	hot-test
crust	spilt	fat
hon-est		fat-ter
	build	fat-test

'If you want to be the best football team, you must trust me and train hard,' said Herbie. And so he kept us at it.

One Thursday, as usual, we went on a run in Green Park. The whole team went together. Skylark, Curly, Corky, Smarty, Sparky, Cartwheel and I, the captain, all went on a run together. Oh, we were hot. It must have been the hottest day of the summer.

'Oh, oh, oh,' wailed Corky. 'I am so hot. I will melt into the dust. I feel limp and damp. I have never felt so sick, so perfectly sick.'

And Curly bent over and wept. 'I never want to run or jump or play football ever again,' she sobbed.

But Herbie was quick to deal with the problem.

'Come on,' he yelled to his football team, the Piggy Porkers. 'Come on. I know you are fed up with the heat. I know you are hot and sticky from a hard run in the sun. But you will feel better when you have had a banana milk shake. Here you are, all of you, a big mug of banana milk shake.'

'Oh,' said Curly, 'that makes me feel better.'

The Green Parkers

(Initial 'ch' and final 'ch' and 'tch')

chap	catch	itch
chat	match	ditch
chain	patch	kitch-en
chase	satch-el	pitch
check	scratch	rich
chest	snatch	sand-wich
cheat		which
cheek	arch	witch
cheese	march	
chick-en		inch
chill	fetch	pinch
chim-ney	stretch	
chin		ap-proach
chip	bench	coach
chief	wrench	poach
chi-na		
chop	each	crutch
choke	beach	hutch
chose	peach	much
chub-by	reach	such
chuck	screech	
chum	teach	

Cross patch,
Shut the latch,
Sit by the fire and spin.
Take a cup
And drink it up
Then call your neighbours in.

How much wood would a woodchuck chuck,
If a woodchuck could chuck wood?

I have a cup of milk at tea,
And some toast and jam.
Tom has his milk in a mug
And eggs and peas and ham.

So we all sat on a bench in the shade. We each drank as much milk shake as we liked. And Herbie gave us each as many sandwiches as we liked. There were cheese sandwiches and chicken sandwiches, and there were chips, too.

'Oh, I feel much better now,' said Corky. 'Me, too,' said Curly. 'Much, much better. Such a lot of yummy chips.'

At that moment, the top football team of all, the Green Parkers, marched into the park. They marched under an arch on their way to train in Green Park.

'A match, a match,' screeched the Piggy Porkers. Curly wrote a note on a scrap of paper. She ran up and gave it to the captain of the Green Parkers.

The note said: 'The Piggy Porkers invite the Green Parkers to a football match next Tuesday at two o'clock on the Piggy Porkers' pitch.'

'OK,' snapped the captain. 'OK, we will play. But you do not have a hope against us. We are the best.'

Sing, sing, what shall I sing?

bang   bank
fang   blanket
hang   prank
sang   tank
       thank

bring
ring   ink
sing   chink
spring   drink
string   link
thing   think

long   monk
prong   monkey
song
strong   sunk
wrong   trunk

clung
sung
swung
tongue
young

Now who is this knocking
At Cottontail's door?
Tap tappit. Tap tappit.
She's heard it before.

Sing a song of sixpence,
A pocket full of rye.
Four and twenty blackbirds
Baked in a pie.

Little children skip,
The rope so gaily gripping.
Tom and Harry
Jane and Mary
Kate, Diana
Susan, Anna,
All are fond of skipping.

Sing a song of pockets.
A pocket full of stones.
A pocket full of feathers,
Or maybe chicken bones.

Tom, Tom, the piper's son
He learned to play
When he was young.
But all the tune that he did play
Was 'Over the hills and far away'.

A rabbit came hopping, hopping,
Hopping along in the park.
'I've just been shopping, shopping,
I must be home before dark.'

In the far corner
Close by the swings
Every morning
A blackbird sings.

Sing, sing, what shall I sing?
The cat has eaten the pudding string.

The Queen of Hearts
She made some tarts
All on a summer's day.
The Knave of Hearts
He stole the tarts,
He stole them clean away.

To market, to market
To buy a fat pig.
Home again, home again
Jiggedy jig.

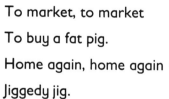

A birdy with a yellow bill
Hopped upon my window sill
Cocked his shining eye and said,
'Ain't you ashamed, you sleepy head?'

Section

This section introduces further vowel combinations and sounds; the final 'le' (as in 'little'); and further effects of 'r' on vowels and vowel combinations.

Teacher's notes

Explain to the child:

(p.84) the sound of double 'o' as in 'zoo' and how other 'o' combinations can sound the same: 'shoe', 'soup', 'do'.

(p.86 and 88) that many different letter combinations sound like 'aw' in 'paw': 'au' in 'Paul', 'daughter' and 'naughty'; 'ou' in 'bought', 'fought' and so on.

(p.90 and 92) how the final 'le' sounds, as in 'lit-tle'.

(p.94) how 'ow' and 'ou' sound in 'cow' and 'loud'. Later (p.100) explain how 'ow' and 'ou' can sound in 'bowl' and 'dough'.

(p.96) further effects of 'r', on vowels as in 'chair', 'fire' and 'floor'. (p.98) how 'oi' and 'oy' sound.

(p.102) that 'o' can be long as in 'bold' and (p.104) that 'i' can be long as in 'child'.

The match begins

(The sound of 'oo')

too	stoop
zoo	goose
	loose
bam-boo	roost
ig-loo	hoot
sham-poo	root
tat-too	shoot
	smooth
food	Hoo-ver
mood	ooze
cool	snooze
fool	choose
pool	
school	do
stool	two
tool	who
broom	can-oe
zoom	shoe
bal-loon	lose
moon	whose
soon	you
spoon	soup
hoop	youth

Shoe the horse, shoe the horse.
Shoe the bay mare.
Here a nail, there a nail,
Still, she stands there.

Sally go round the sun,
Sally go round the moon,
Sally go round the chimney-pots,
On a Saturday afternoon.

It was soon time for the big match. Two o'clock on Tuesday came in no time at all.

'Too soon for me,' muttered Corky.

'Oo,' moaned Curly. 'Oo, I wish we did not have to play against the Green Parkers. I must be a fool to have had this idea. Everybody knows they are the best team in the whole world.'

The match began. Stan the Stork was the referee. 'As soon as I blow my horn the game can start,' he said.

Zoom, the two teams whizzed up and down the pitch. Lots of fans had come. The chimpanzees yelled and yelled for their friends the Piggy Porkers. They waved big blue balloons with 'Up the Piggy Porkers' written on them in pink letters.

Who was going to shoot the first goal? Which team was going to win? Who was going to lose?

The Piggy Porkers score a goal

(The sound of 'au' and 'aw')

claw
draw
jaw
law
paw
raw
saw
see-saw
straw

hawk

bawl
crawl
shawl
haul
sprawl

lawn
prawn
yawn

aw-ful
awk-ward

Au-gust
au-tumn
caught
daugh-ter
naugh-ty
slaugh-ter

fault
som-er-sault

haunt
jaunt

di-no-saur
Lau-ra

be-cause
Santa Claus

ex-hausted

'We will beat you up,' bawled the Green Parkers' fan club. 'We will slaughter you. You will crawl away into a ditch when we have finished with you.'

They were cross because they saw the Piggy Porkers doing well. They were cross because they, the Green Parkers, were the famous team. How awful if they were beaten by this silly team of pigs.

The Piggy Porkers' fans were going mad. What fun. What a thrill. 'Up the Piggy Porkers. Win, win, win,' they bawled.

Then Corky saw the goal net free. In a flash

she had scored a goal. Stan the Stork yelled, 'Piggy Porkers, one; Green Parkers, nil.'

Suddenly, Naughty Nora, one of the Green Parkers, stuck out her leg and caught Skylark's leg. Skylark did a somersault and went sprawling on the pitch.

Luckily the referee saw what happened. Luckily Stan the Stork saw it was Naughty Nora's fault.

'I saw you, Naughty Nora,' he said. 'Skylark's fall was your fault. I saw you trip her up. I saw you send her sprawling. You must leave the pitch. You must be taught a lesson.'

Naughty Nora is sent off

(The sound of 'al', 'ar', 'ou', etc)

all
ball
call
fall
hall
small
wall

false
al-so

bald
scald

halt
salt

al-most
al-though
al-ways

wal-nut

war
a-ward
re-ward
ward-robe
dwarf
warm
swarm

wa-ter

chalk
stalk
talk
walk

ought
bought
brought
fought
nought
thought

So Naughty Nora had to leave the pitch. Stan the Stork also gave her a ticket and talked to her.

'You have brought shame on your team again, Naughty Nora,' he said. 'You always do something bad. Go and sit by the wall.'

Skylark's fall made the Piggy Porkers try all the more. They fought and fought to get the ball and score again. And they did. Suddenly the Piggy Porkers had two goals and the Green Parkers had none.

Then Stan the Stork called, 'Time up. End of match. The score is Piggy Porkers, two; Green Parkers, nought. The winners are the Piggy Porkers. Now let's all have a long drink of water.'

Mummy, may I go and swim?
Yes, my darling daughter.
Hang your clothes on a hawthorn tree.
And don't go in the water.

Ferry me across the water,
Do, Boatman, do.
If you've a penny in your purse
I'll ferry you.

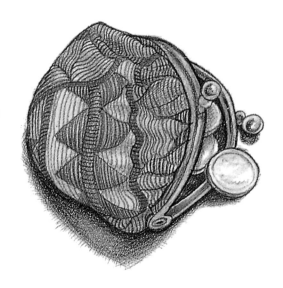

Humpty Dumpty sat on a wall.
Humpty Dumpty had a great fall.
All the king's horses and all the king's men
Couldn't put Humpty together again.

Miss Penny Pig's story ends

(The final 'le')

a-ble   poss-i-ble   bat-tle
sta-ble   cat-tle
ta-ble   cra-dle   prat-tle
fee-ble   la-dle   rat-tle
no-ble   nee-dle   ket-tle
           i-dle   net-tle
                        set-tle
bab-ble
dab-ble   sad-dle   lit-tle
peb-ble   med-dle   scut-tle
nib-ble   fid-dle
scrib-ble mid-dle   star-tle
bob-ble   rid-dle   tur-tle
bub-ble   cod-dle
           hud-dle
am-ble   mud-dle
bram-ble   pud-dle
ram-ble
thim-ble   can-dle
grum-ble   handle
jum-ble   kin-dle
mum-ble   fon-dle
           bun-dle

'And so,' says Miss Penny Pig, 'that is my story. That is the way the Piggy Porkers' team, that everybody thought was little and feeble, was able to beat the best. That is the way we were able to become the champions of all.

'I think we startled the Green Parkers by the way we were able to handle the ball. They got into an awful muddle and we won the match. We beat the team who were unbeaten. They thought they were unbeatable but they were not.

'And that is the end of my story.'

Jack be nimble,
Jack be quick,
Jack jump over
The candle stick.

Riddle me ree,
Riddle me ree,
The cat's run away
With the bumble bee.

Old Mother Shuttle
Lived in a coal scuttle
Along with her dog and her cat.
What they ate I can't tell,
But 'tis known very well
That not one of that party was fat.

Hark, the wind. Oh, how it whistles,
Through the trees and flowers and thistles.

Miss Penny Pig needs to gargle

(More final 'le')

trea-cle   cac-kle
            tac-kle
sti-fle   frec-kle
tri-fle   spec-kle
            pic-kle
duf-fle   tric-kle
shuf-fle   buc-kle
snuf-fle   knuc-kle

Of speckled eggs the birdie sings
And nests among the trees;
The sailor sings of ropes and things
In ships upon the seas.

bea-gle   ap-ple
ea-gle   crip-ple
bu-gle   sup-ple

An apple a day
Keeps the doctor away.

gag-gle   tram-ple
wrig-gle   sim-ple
tog-gle   crum-ple
smug-gle

            peo-ple
jun-gle   pur-ple
gar-gle
gur-gle   daz-zle
            driz-zle
twin-kle   puz-zle

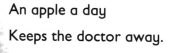

Twinkle, twinkle, little star,
How I wonder what you are!
Up above the world so high,
Like a diamond in the sky.

'Well,' says Miss Penny Pig. 'I have talked so much that my throat is quite sore. I think I will have a little gargle. Is there some gargle?'

'Oh, yes,' cackles Jen the Hen. 'I have some gargle. I always make rose hip syrup every autumn for sore throats and snuffles. My simple rose hip syrup is the best thing to tackle a sore throat.'

And Jen the Hen gives a little wriggle and a shuffle and from the very bottom of her pocket brings out a little bottle. On the little bottle is a label which says in big red letters:

Jen the Hen's Sore Throat and Snuffle Gargle. Trickle a little into a cup. Add a little water and gargle four times a day.

Jen the Hen trickles a little into a cup, adds a little water and Miss Penny Pig gargles. 'Gurgle, gurgle, gurgle,' she says. 'Thank you, Jen. That is much better.'

The train stops

(The sound of 'ou' and 'ow')

cow	loud	count
now	a-loud	count-er
how	cloud	count-y
sow	proud	fount-ain
bow		mount-ain
	owl	
plough	howl	hound
bough	fowl	found
drought	growl	sound
	scowl	round
mouth	tow-el	a-round
south		
house	town	our
mouse	down	flour
	drown	sour
out	crown	flow-er
pout	frown	pow-er
shout	brown	show-er
stout	clown	tow-er
trout		
a-bout	pouch	
	crouch	

'Our train has stopped. We are in a town,' shouts Tab the Cat. 'I can see houses. I can see thousands of houses and crowds of people. I can tell our train has stopped because there is no more clatter of the wheels going round and round. I'm getting out.'

'I shall get out of the train, too. I shall have a walk about the town,' shouts Freddy the Frog.

'I shall take my towel with me in case I see some water to swim in. It would be fun if I found a fountain to shower me with water. My skin has got very dry because I have been out of water for so long.'

Oh, the grand old Duke of York,

He had ten thousand men,

He marched them up to the top of the hill,

And he marched them down again.

And when they were up they were up,

And when they were down they were down,

And when they were only half-way up,

They were neither up nor down.

Doctor Foster

Went to Glo'ster

In a shower of rain;

He stepped in a puddle

Right up to his middle

And never went there again.

I wish how I wish that I had a little house,

With a mat for the cat and a holey for a mouse,

And a clock going tock in a corner of the room,

And a kettle, and a cupboard and a big birch broom.

Freddy the Frog on the railway line

(The sound of 'air', 'ear', 'fire', 'roar' and 'cure')

air   fire   cure
air-port   hire   pure
chair   tire   crea-ture
fair   tyre   fu-ture
hair   wire   mix-ture
care   spire   na-ture
dare   pir-ate   pic-ture
share

spare   boar   air
stare   oar   bear
    roar   their
dear   broad   there
ear   a-broad   where
deer   door
beer   more
hear   sore
fear   core
near   score
year   floor
clear   four
cheer   pour
steer   your
here

'Oh dear, oh dear,' wails Freddy the Frog, as he steps down on to the platform. 'I have dropped my towel on to the track. But it is quite near the side and the line seems clear. I cannot hear a train coming. If I take care I am sure it will be easy for me to get down on to the track and pick up my towel. I am sure I can steer clear of all those electric wires.'

So Freddy the Frog begins to let himself down over the side of the platform to get his towel.

But suddenly, zoom, an enormous express train comes thundering out of nowhere.

'Oh, oh, oh,' yells Freddy the Frog. 'Help me, save me. Spare me, you horrid train.'

'Clear the track, you frantic frog,' yells the train driver. 'Don't you see that I cannot stop? It takes a train over a mile to stop. A train cannot stop when it likes, you know.'

Just then something amazing happens. There is a great rush like a whirlwind. Freddy the Frog is scooped up and finds himself safe and sound back on the platform, well clear of the train.

Freddy the Frog finds himself staring at a big, tall creature, all in blue.

'Well,' says the big, tall creature. 'Well, Freddy the Frog, what have you to say for yourself?'

Tab the Cat is thirsty

(The sound of 'oi' and 'oy')

boy   a-hoy
joy   an-noy
toy   de-coy
           de-stroy
boil   en-joy
coil   soy-a
foil   roy-al
soil   oy-ster
spoil
toil

a-void
join
joint
oint-ment
point
noise
poi-son

'Er... thank you very much,' says Freddy the Frog. 'I ought not to have done that, I suppose.' And he sits down quickly because his legs feel like jelly.

'That train very nearly crushed you, you frantic frog,' says the big, tall creature in blue. 'There was so much noise around on the noisy platform that it drowned the noise of the express train. It is lucky I was there to save you. Remember, keep off railway lines.' And the creature in blue zooms off.

Meanwhile, Tab the Cat, who has gone for a walk round the town, has found a bottle by the side of the road.

'Oh, it is hot,' he says. 'Oh, I do want a drink. I am so thirsty. And here is a nice bottle. I expect it is lemonade. There are some funny letters on the label. P-O-I-S-O-N. Now I wonder what that can mean. Perhaps it is a new sort of lemonade I have never tasted. Well, I am so thirsty I will try it now.'

And Tab the Cat lifts the bottle to his lips.

Ladybird, ladybird, fly away home.
Your house is on fire and your children all gone.
All but one and her name is Ann
And she crept under the frying pan.

What are little boys made of?
What are little boys made of?
Slugs and snails and puppy dogs' tails,
That's what little boys are made of.

Girls and boys
Come out to play.
The moon does shine
As bright as day.

Tweedledum and Tweedledee
Agreed to have a battle;
For Tweedledum said Tweedledee
Had spoiled his nice new rattle.

Tab nearly drinks poison

('ow' and 'ou' can sound like long 'o')

bow	owe	found
crow		pound
know	bowl	sound
low		
mow	own	bow
show	owner	cow
slow		how
snow	known	now
throw	thrown	sow
win-dow	be-low	howl
el-bow	low-er	owl
	low-est	
shal-low		frown
bel-low	dough	brown
fel-low	though	drown
yellow		
bil-low	cloud	
pil-low		
wil-low	bough	
hol-low		

spar-row

Zoom. Wallop.

Just as Tab the Cat is about to drink from the bottle it is knocked from his hand. A big, tall creature in blue suddenly swoops down on him in a cloud of smoke.

'Hey, you silly fellow,' he bellows. 'Do you know what is in that bottle? Show it to me. Can you read the label? It says POISON. That means it is very, very bad for you. It might even kill you. Let me throw it away. Never, never drink something unless you know for sure it is all right. Goodbye for now.'

And the big, tall creature in blue zooms off in a cloud.

Rock-a-bye baby, on the tree top;
When the wind blows the cradle will rock;
When the bough breaks the cradle will fall;
Down will come baby, cradle and all.

Who killed Cock Robin?
I, said the sparrow,
With my bow and arrow
I killed Cock Robin.

Who saw him die?
I, said the fly,
With my little eye
I saw him die.

When I was sick and lay abed,
I had two pillows at my head,
And all my toys about me lay
To keep me happy all the day.

A postcard home

(The long sound of 'o')

bold   on-ly

cold

fold   don't

gold   won't

hold

old   most

sold   post

told

post-box

gold-fish   post-card

sol-di-er

soul

roll

boul-der

shoul-der

oak

folk

yolk

'Gosh,' says Tab the Cat. 'I won't do that again. I won't try to drink from a bottle I don't know again. Lucky for me that big, tall creature in blue was around. Lucky for me he told me not to drink it. Silly old bottle. I only hope it has rolled a long way away.

'Oh, I can see a post-box. I must send a postcard home to tell my family where I am. If I found a shop which sold a postcard I could send a note to all the people at home.

'There is Freddy the Frog. Hey, Freddy, my dear old frog, what are you up to? Have you had your swim? You told me you were going for a swim to make your skin wet and cold. You told us a frog must keep his skin as cold and wet as possible.

'The most awful thing happened to me, Freddy, my dear old frog. It was the most awful thing, but luckily I was saved by the most amazing big, tall creature all in blue.'

Big Ben strikes
Not when he likes
But when he is told to.

A pair of shoes
Never can choose
Who to be sold to.

We have a little garden,
A garden of our own.
And every day we water there
The seeds that we have sown.

Don't Care was made to care;
Don't Care was hung;
Don't Care was put in a pot
And boiled till he was done.

We want to swim

(The long sound of 'i')

night	child
bright	mild
fight	wild
flight	
fright	wild-ness
light	
might	climb
right	
sight	be-hind
slight	bind
tight	blind
	find
frigh-ten	grind
	mind
day-light	rind
de-light	unkind
moon-light	wind
sun-light	
	blind-ness
over-night	kind-ness
height	pint
	Heinz

'Well, Tab the Cat,' says Freddy the Frog, 'I was saved by exactly the same kind of person. I had the most awful fright, too. It was quite the most awful fright of my whole life. Luckily for me, this big, tall creature in blue must have been right behind me. He saw me climb down on to the railway line.

'Oh, I was frightened. The bright lights of the train suddenly came at me. I shall never forget the sight and the sound of the train. And then, whoosh, I find I am safe. And this kind person did not seem to mind very much. I mean, he might have been wild.

'But no, I did not find a place to swim. I shall die if I do not have a swim. My skin feels dry and tight. Let us see if we can find some water right away. I shall ask that child in a white hat.

'Excuse me, do you mind telling me the way to the nearest swimming pool?'

Snail upon the wall,
Have you got at all
Anything to tell
About your shell?

Only this, my child —
When the wind is wild,
Or when the sun is hot,
It's all I've got.

The friendly cow all red and white
I love with all my heart.
She gives me cream with all her might
To eat with apple tart.

In winter I get up at night
And dress by yellow candlelight. ·
In summer quite the other way,
I have to go to bed by day.

I have to go to bed and see
The birds still hopping on the tree,
Or hear the grown-up people's feet
Still going past me in the street.

Hey diddle, diddle,
The cat and the fiddle,
The cow jumped over the moon.
The little dog laughed to see such fun
And the dish ran away with the spoon.

Section

This section introduces more odd vowel sounds; the soft 'c' as in 'ice'; and the soft 'g' as in 'cottage'.

Teacher's notes

Explain to the child:

(p.108) that 'o' and 'ou' can sound like a short 'u': 'son', 'rough'. (p.110) that 'or' and 'our' can sound like 'ur': 'worm', 'colour'.

(p.112) the sound of the short 'u' as in 'push'.

(p.114) that 'oo' can sound short as in 'foot'; also 'o' and 'ou' can sound like the 'oo' in 'foot': 'woman', 'could'.

(p.116) that 'a' can sound broad as in 'class' and 'ew' like 'u' as in 'new'. (p.118) that 'ea' can sound short as in 'tread' and 'ear' can sound like 'er'.

(p.120) that 'c' followed by 'e', 'i' or 'y' can sound like 's': 'circle', 'face'.

(p.122) that 'g' sounds like 'j' before 'e' and 'i': 'large', 'giant'.

A little nut tree

('o' and 'ou' sound like the short 'u' of 'mud')

doub-le   Lon-don
troub-le   Mon-day
cous-in   mon-ey
coun-try   hon-ey
coup-le   tongue
young   a-mong
e-nough   mon-key
tough   come
rough   some
touch

               broth-er
love   moth-er
dove   oth-er
a-bove   noth-ing
shove
love-ly   does
               doz-en
son   wor-ry
ton
won
won-der
one
done

I had a little nut tree,
Nothing would it bear,
But a silver nutmeg
And a golden pear.

The King of Spain's daughter
Came to visit me,
And all for the sake
Of my little nut tree.

Someone came knocking
At my wee small door;
Someone came knocking,
I'm sure, sure, sure.

I'm a little rabbit
In my rabbit hutch.
You can come and touch me,
But please don't clutch.

Diddle, diddle dumpling, my son John
Went to bed with his trousers on.
One shoe off and one shoe on.
Diddle, diddle dumpling, my son John.

Old Mother Hubbard went to the cupboard
To get her poor dog a bone;
But when she got there the cupboard was bare
And so the poor dog had none.

Digging for worms

('or' and 'our' sound like 'ur')

word

work

world

worm

worse

worth

work-er

work-shop

mot-or

rot-or

sail-or

tail-or

lab-our

neigh-bour

col-our

parl-our

fav-our-ite

'My word,'

Said Bill Bird,

'Have you heard,

At our Sports Day I came third?

Puss came first

With a burst.

Rat was worst;

How he cursed!

But my word, how Puss purred.'

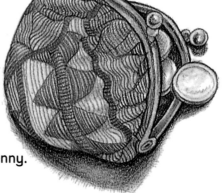

I'll sing you a song,

Though not very long,

Yet I think it as pretty as any.

Put your hand in your purse,

You'll never be worse,

And give the poor singer a penny.

I had a dog and his name was Dandy,

His tail was long and his legs were bandy,

His eyes were brown and his coat was sandy,

The best dog in the world was my dog Dandy.

'I cannot stop,' says the child. 'I have work to do.'

'Work?' say Tab the Cat and Freddy the Frog. 'Work? You are too young to work.'

'Oh, no,' says the child. 'I dig for worms. I am very busy digging up worms. My worms are worth a lot of money. People use my worms to catch fish. You see, we are very near the river here. People on their way to the river to fish stop and buy my worms.

'My favourite worm is this brown striped one. But that horrid black one is the worst sort of worm in the whole world.'

'River?' shouts Freddy the Frog. 'Where?'

'Oh, the river is very near,' says the child. 'It's just down the road.' So Freddy the Frog and Tab the Cat run down the road towards the river.

A swim in the river

(The sound of the short 'u')

pud-ding

bull
full
pull

bush
cush-ion
push

puss
pussy

butch-er
put

pain-ful
care-ful
grate-ful
play-ful

beau-ti-ful

Pussy cat, Pussy cat, where have you been?
I've been up to London to visit the queen.
Pussy cat, Pussy cat, what did you there?
I frightened a little mouse under her chair.

Pease pudding hot,
Pease pudding cold,
Pease pudding in the pot,
Nine days old.

Polly put the kettle on,
Polly put the kettle on,
Polly put the kettle on,
We'll all have tea.

Old Mr Prickle-pin
Has never a cushion to stick his pins in;
His nose is black and his beard is grey,
And he lives in an ash stump over the way.

'Oh, beautiful, wonderful river,' cries Freddy the Frog. 'I am glad to see you. I shall put my things behind this bush and jump straight in.'

'But Freddy the Frog. Over there, see, there is a sign. I wonder what it says. Can you read it?'

'Sign? What sign? Something silly, I expect,' says Freddy the Frog.

But the sign on the other side of the river is not silly at all. It says: NO SWIMMING – DEEP WATER – STRONG CURRENTS. 'Freddy, what is a strong current?' cries Tab the Cat. But it's too late. Freddy the Frog comes up behind Tab the Cat and pushes him in.

'But Freddy,' shouts Tab the Cat, 'I can't swim.' And he falls like a stone into the cold dark water and sinks to the bottom.

Rescue from the river

(The sound of the short 'oo' and 'ou' as in 'foot')

good   wolf
hood   wolves
stood
wood   woman

book   could
brook   should
cook   would
hook
look
rook
shook
took

wool

foot
soot

foot-ball
bare-foot
flat-foot-ed
good-look-ing

Suddenly, whoosh, there is a great rush and whirl and Tab the Cat feels himself being pulled up. Someone gets hold of his foot and pulls him out of the water. Someone puts a big hook round Tab the Cat's foot and gives it a good pull.

Safe again on dry land, Tab the Cat shakes the water from his ears and takes a good look at the person who has saved him. It is a big, tall, good-looking creature in blue.

'Well,' he says to Tab the Cat. 'It is lucky I was around to hook you out. You would have drowned if I had not pulled you out. But you should not have been in the water if you cannot swim. And look over there. Look at that sign on the other side of the river. That sign is to tell you this river is not safe.'

'As for you, you flat-footed frog, you should never, never push.'

'I know, I know,' says Freddy the Frog. 'I do not know how I could have been so stupid. Please forgive me, Tab the Cat.

'You see, ever since I was a tadpole I have been able to swim. And so, because I am a good swimmer, I suppose I think everybody else can swim well too.'

'Goodbye,' says the big, tall, good-looking creature in blue. 'I must be off now. I have work to do.'

'Thank you, thank you,' say Tab the Cat and Freddy the Frog. 'But who are you?'

But he has gone.

Who is the mystery man?

('a' sounds like 'ar' and 'ew' like 'u')

glass	ask	clasp
grass	flask	
pass	task	bath
class	bask-et	fa-ther
brass		
	calf	new
last	half	flew
past	laugh	chew
fast		dew
cast	calm	stew
cast-le	palm	knew
mast		blew
mast-er	aunt	
dis-ast-er	can't	
plast-er	shan't	
ghast-ly	chant	
	grant	
aft-er	slant	
raft		
shaft	ba-na-na	
	py-ja-ma	
	an-swer	
	branch	

'I can't tell you who that wonderful mystery man is,' says Freddy the Frog. 'I wish I knew.

'You can't ask him. And so you can't get an answer. I tried to ask last time after he saved me from the railway track. But he always zooms off so fast there is no time to ask him his name. And no time for an answer.

'But he is the most super mystery man in the world. He has saved me from a ghastly disaster. And he has saved you from two ghastly disasters. And we can't even ask him his name.

'I wish I knew.'

My mother said
That I never should
Play with the gypsies
In the wood.
If I did, she would say,
'Naughty girl to disobey.'

Baa, baa, black sheep,
Have you any wool?
Yes, sir, yes, sir,
Three bags full.

One for the master,
One for the dame,
And one for the little boy
Who lives down the lane.

There was an old woman tossed up in a basket
Nineteen times as high as the moon.
Where she was going, I couldn't but ask it,
For in her hand she carried a broom.

Freddy the Frog is hungry

(The short 'ea' as in 'bread' and 'ear' sounding like 'er')

bread	sweat
dead	
head	breath
in-stead	death
read-y	feath-er
stead-y	leath-er
spread	weath-er
tread	
thread	heav-en
deaf	search
break-fast	heard
dealt	ear-ly
jeal-ous	pearl
meant	earn
	learn
leapt	
	earth
breast	earth-quake
pleas-ant	earth-worm

As Tab the Cat and Freddy the Frog run along the road back to the train, Freddy the Frog says, 'Ooh, I can smell fresh bread. Yum, yum. Where is that lovely smell of fresh bread coming from? Oh, I can see. There is a baker's shop across the road. Look over there, Tab the Cat.'

'No, no,' puffs Tab the Cat, already out of breath. 'We have no time to buy bread. Are you deaf? The train's whistle has already blown. I heard it. The train is ready to go and we are not yet on it. It will not be very pleasant to be left here instead of going to Spain with the rest of our friends.'

'There's masses of time,' says greedy Freddy the Frog. 'I'm going to dash quickly across the road to get some bread for breakfast. I'll get some for Miss Penny Pig and the others as well or they'll be jealous. I shan't be a tick. I'll just dash across the road.'

How do you like to go up in a swing?
Up in the air so blue?
Oh, I do think it the pleasantest thing
Ever a child can do.

Well, I never
Did you ever
See a monkey
Dressed in leather;
Leather eyes
Leather nose
Leather breeches
To his toes?

When the weather is wet
We must not fret.

A robin redbreast in a cage
Puts all heaven in a rage.

Freddy is saved from an accident

('c' before 'e', 'i' or 'y' sounds like 's')

ce-real   face   dance

ceil-ing   lace   France

cell   race   prance

cer-tain   space

dis-grace   fence

cin-e-ma   pence

circ-le   peace   si-lence

cir-cus   fleece   ab-sence

cit-y   piece

niece   mince

cyc-le   prince

cym-bal   police   prin-cess

re-ceive   ice   once

par-cel   mice

ex-cept   nice   dunce

sau-cer   rice

slice   ounce

ac-ci-dent   spice   bounce

pen-cil   twice

ex-cite

voice

juic-y

'Oh, no,' cries Tab the Cat. 'Calm down, Freddy the Frog, and don't get so excited about a silly old loaf of bread. Look out or there will be an accident. That big cereal van will hit you. Oh, I cannot face it. That cereal van will cut you into millions of little pieces. Oh, Freddy, you will be minced up.'

Poor Tab the Cat puts his paws over his face. He is certain there is going to be a horrid accident. He is certain there is going to be a horrid circle of squashed frog in the middle of the road.

'I can face anything except that,' sobs Tab the Cat. And then, whoosh. The big, tall creature in blue comes to the rescue again. He swoops down and sweeps Freddy the Frog out of the path of the big cereal van.

Freddy the Frog is safe and sound on the pavement beside Tab the Cat. They dance and prance with joy.

Go to bed late,
Stay very small;
Go to bed early,
Grow very tall.

Milk is nice for Monday,
Milk begins with M.
Treacle tarts for Tuesday,
I'm very fond of them.
Walnuts do for Wednesday,
Thursday toast and tea,
Friday fish and
Saturday soup,
And Sunday wait and see.

Three blind mice, three blind mice,
See how they run, see how they run;
They all ran after the farmer's wife
Who cut off their tails with a carving knife,
Did you ever see such a thing in your life
As three blind mice?

The Danger Ranger

(Soft 'g' before 'e', and 'i')

gent-le   an-gel   fringe
ge-ni-us   change   singe
           dan-ger
gi-ant   ran-ger   sponge
gin-ger   stran-ger
gip-sy   dun-geon
gi-raffe   barge   plunge
           charge

age   large   badge
cage   mag-ic
page   merge
rage   verge   edge
                     hedge

dam-age   forge
man-age   gorge   fid-get
gar-age   pig-eon
saus-age   huge   por-ridge

cab-bage   urge   dodge
lug-gage   surge   lodge
vil-lage
mes-sage   en-gine   budge
cot-tage   judge

'Gosh,' says Freddy the Frog to the large blue giant who has saved him. 'Gosh, I mean thank you; you are a genius. I mean a very large thank you. I mean a huge, huge thank you, Mr... I am very sorry, I do not know your name. I am a stranger here. My friend, Tab the Cat, and I are strangers here.'

'Well, Freddy the Frog and Tab the Cat, I am the Danger Ranger. It is my job to charge about all over the place and save people from danger. It is my job to keep foolish frogs and crazy cats out of danger. It is my job to keep them from doing damage to themselves.

'You two have kept me very busy. First you, Freddy the Frog, when you plunged over the edge of the platform to get your towel. Then you, Tab the Cat, with that large bottle of poison. You were about to do huge damage to your insides. But luckily I managed to stop you.